THE SEASONS OF A
WOMAN'S LIFE

D'Ann V. Johnson

THE SEASONS OF A WOMAN'S LIFE
Copyright © 2019 by D'Ann V. Johnson

ISBN-13: 978-0-9792414-4-4

Unless otherwise indicated, Scripture quotations are from The Holy Bible, New King James Version (NKJV), copyright © 1982 by Thomas Nelson, Inc.

Published by Psalmist & Scribe Publishing, Inc. (www.psalmistandscribe.com)

Cover design and layout by Vivian Fisher, Concept, Inc. Ellenwood, GA

Editorial services rendered by Tawni Fears (www.info@TawniLogues.com)

Acknowledgements

Whenever I consider a work of ministry or creativity, I immediately think about the great encourager in my life, my husband, Pastor Billy R. Johnson. For more than thirty years, this man has seen in me what I have been unable to see in myself. In this particular stage of my life, he has amped up his push, convincing me that the transition into my new season is not only possible, but it is bright and beautiful. For that, and more importantly, for him, I remain eternally grateful.

I must also give a special shout-out to our adult son, Stephen, in whom I see his father's characteristics more and more. When he was born, I declared him to be my "joy and blessing," and he continues to be just that. Each time I complete a book or fulfill some portion of my vision, he beams with genuine pride that makes me wonder what I did to gain the honor of being his mother.

I recently gave a gift to my dear friend, Vivian Fisher, called "The Key to Success" because that is what she has been for me. More years ago than I can remember, she invested her extraordinary graphic skills in designing three book jackets. Each one represented a title I told her I believed were books I was supposed to write. She wrapped them around blank journals, put them on beautiful stands, and presented them to me as a gift to remind me that I was born to write. Now many years later, she has brought my vision to pass for every book, message cover, logo, conference, and more. What I can convey verbally, she amplifies visually. She makes everything that I do better than it could ever be alone. I know God has a special reward for her kindness.

I am blessed with a wonderful team of women who surround me with their wisdom and confidence in my calling. I love and appreciate the investment that these "soul sisters" continue to make to ensure that the will of God is fulfilled through me. Thank you, Andrea Nettles, Arnita Davis, Jacquelyn Gardner, and LaVonne Smith, for always bringing your best and for getting the best out of me. May we continue to live in the overflow together.

With a heart filled with gratitude, I must acknowledge Babbie Mason and Cynthia L. Hale's kindness for writing the forewords to this book. Having more than one introduction to a written work may not be customary. Still, it was necessary for me as these are two women I respect, admire, and count myself privileged to know personally. As I have watched them use their unique gifts for the glory of God, my life has been enriched. Little did they know they were teaching me how to live before others and in faithfulness to the God we know and love.

This book is dedicated to all the women in my life who have lived before me in power and authenticity. Our relationships spread across family, church, ministry, corporate America, and even the mall. I am a better woman because of each of you, far too numerous to name, but always in my heart.

Everything that I am and anything good that comes through me is because of the One who knows me best and loves me most. The best of me is because of Christ in me, and that relationship continues to be the most important and vital one of my life. May you, Father God, always be pleased and receive glory.

Gratefully,

Dr. D'

Table of Contents

A Foreword from
Babbie Mason

For many women, the thought of advancing through the seasons of life to face inevitable change can be overwhelming and daunting. For one woman, she wonders if she will ever find Mr. Right, who she dreams will sweep her off her feet and fulfill her hopes of getting married and starting a family. For another, it seems that only yesterday her child was mouthing his first words, but seemingly overnight, that same kid morphed into a mouthy teenager who is an authority on everything. For another woman, she remembers the exciting days of launching and building her own business, traveling, and meeting new people, but down the road and around the bend, she faces the reality of an economic downturn and an overdrawn bank account. Then there is yet another woman whose home once burgeoned with the day-to-day episodes of a growing family, the security of a strong marriage, mortgage payments, baseball games, and piano recitals, who now finds herself living alone in her senior years, startled by the echo of deafening silence in her empty nest.

Whether one of these scenarios describes your life or you are somewhere in between, the seasons of life can leave you exhausted, emotionally drained, or questioning the future. But here is the reassuring truth of it all. No one knows more about the season you are in better than your heavenly Father, the One who spoke every season into existence.

No matter what age or stage you find yourself in, it is imperative for women to huddle around the communal fires where we can talk about the real issues of life. Sitting at the center of our circle of friends, helping her counterparts find the way to healing and wholeness, is Dr. D'Ann Johnson, the author of this great book, The Seasons of a Woman's Life.

Dr. D'Ann Johnson and I go way back. My memories of her date as far back as the eighties, so I have been taking notes on her for over thirty years. I knew her long before she was known as Dr. D', and long before she was the executive pastor of New Covenant Christian Ministries, where she serves alongside her husband, Pastor Billy R. Johnson. Through the years, I have observed how she balances family, ministry, education, and business, putting her shoulder to the wheel to become a well-established author, an accomplished leader in the church and community, and a persuasive communicator.

For three decades, I have watched her navigate challenges and setbacks only to see her come back stronger for the struggle. I have seen her discover her numerous talents to develop into a multi-gifted and grounded woman whose heart is full of relentless faith in the God she loves. She exudes an undeniable inner resolve, and she is not afraid to tell you where she finds her help. Proverbs 31:25-26 NLT describes her rock-solid confidence in Christ to the letter: "She is clothed with strength and dignity, and she laughs without fear of the future. When she speaks, her words are wise, and she gives instructions with kindness." It is no wonder why Dr. D' is qualified to speak to our hearts on the subject of the seasons of a woman's life.

On the pages of this most timely book, you will discover that as long as you have a pulse, you have a purpose; that there is no expiration date on God's plan for your life; and that every age and every stage of your life has eternal significance.

With no reservation, I highly recommend this powerful book, and I challenge you not only to read its contents but to revel in the eternal truth found on these pages. And when you have read it right down to the last word, you will find your life richer, fuller, deeper, sweeter, and ready to face the uncertain days ahead with victory and joy. Rest assured, God is for you. You are His favorite, and your best and brightest days are still ahead of you.

Babbie Mason
Award-winning Gospel Singer/Songwriter,
Author and Master Mentor
http://babbie.com/
https://www.babbiemasonradio.com/

A Foreword from
Dr. Cynthia L. Hale

Several years ago, I made a wonderful discovery that altered the course of my life. I discovered that, as women, we live our lives in seasons. The writer Qoheleth affirms in Ecclesiastes 3:1, "There is a time for everything and a season for every activity under heaven."

There is a season of childhood, puberty, and youth; a season of education, a season of preparation, a season of developing a career or getting a job, a season of falling in love, and a season of falling out of love; a season of marriage, a season of singleness, a season of doing your own thing and paying dearly for it; a season of insecurity—a lack of confidence and fear, a season of self-awareness, a season of coming into one's own.

There are seasons of grief, seasons of pain, seasons of facing new responsibilities, and seasons of great gain. There is a season of raising children, then releasing them and letting them go; a season of great productivity, a season of reflection and growth; a season of caring for the world, and a season of rest.

This revelation opened my eyes to the endless possibilities of life. It would not allow me to get comfortable, thinking that I had arrived or get stuck in a particular season when there is so much more to experience in the abundant and eternal life God has given us.

Well, I thought I fully understood the richness of living my life in seasons until I was asked to write the foreword to Dr. D's book, The Seasons of a Woman's Life. And now that I have had the privilege of reading it, I know how much more I had to learn.

In her inimitable way, as a master teacher, Dr. D' has excavated the depths of understanding the seasons to help us discern the purpose, possibility, and opportunity that each one provides us. She has skillfully examined biblical passages, lifting the truth for us not only to see ourselves but become as productive as we can be in each season of our lives. She then lovingly pushes us to probe our own inner being through "Season Thoughts" to make sure that we are not simply impressed with her writing (which you will be) but are also impacted by it. I promise you, after reading this book, your life will never be the same again.

Dr. Cynthia L. Hale
Senior Pastor, Ray of Hope Christian Church
President, Women in Ministry Conference, Inc.
Author, I'm a Piece of Work: Sisters Shaped by God
https://cynthialhale.org/

Introduction

Several years ago, I ran across a story about the significance of seasons and how what happens in each is perceived differently. Through the years, I have seen various versions of the story but have been unable to identify its source. Even without knowing its origin, the following is a powerful depiction of the importance of recognizing and embracing each season of life.

The story goes something like this.

A woman had four daughters. She wanted her daughters to learn not to judge things too quickly, so she sent them each on a quest to go and look at a pear tree that was a great distance away. The first daughter went in the winter, the second in the spring, the third in the summer, and the youngest in the fall.

When they had all gone and returned, the mother called them together to describe what they had seen. The first daughter said that the tree was ugly, bent, and twisted. The second daughter disagreed, saying that the tree was covered with green buds and full of promise. The third daughter declared that the previous description was not wholly accurate. She added that the tree was laden with blossoms that smelled sweet and looked so beautiful that it made the tree the most graceful thing she had ever seen. The youngest daughter took issue with them all, stating that the tree was already ripe, drooping with fruit, and full of life and fulfillment.

As the daughters began arguing between themselves as to who gave the most accurate portrayal of the tree, the mother interrupted them. "You are each correct because you each saw the tree in only one season of its life," she said. Sharing the more profound meaning for their explorations, their mother explained further. "Like a tree, we cannot judge a person by only one season. The essence of who they are can only be measured when all their seasons have ended."

Regardless of the variations of how this story has been told, the essential and evident lesson remains the same. If you give up in any season, you will miss the promise of your spring, the beauty of your summer, the fulfillment of your fall, and the clarity of your winter. So regardless of where you currently find your life settling, it is my sincere hope that this book will help you see the importance of every season, the inherent beauty therein, and the promise that awaits you as you gracefully navigate and steward the seasons of your life.

Chapter One:
Stages vs. Seasons

There is a train of thought that suggests that to understand what something is, it is essential to know what it is not. That belief can be tremendously beneficial in grasping the seasons that take place in a person's life. Although possibly unrealized, there are times when, in fact, what we are encountering is only a stage.

A stage is a period or a step in the progression of development. One dictionary describes it as a single step or degree in a process, or a particular phase, period, or position in a process, development, or series.[1]

Each of us has experienced various stages in life. I can still remember the time in my life that would be classified as the "awkward stage." I cannot speak for anyone else, but that was a gruelingly difficult time. I had arms and legs that seemed to swing from an undeveloped and stunted torso and merciless acne that relished in its ability to multiply by the moment. Although that period seemed to last forever, my body parts began to coordinate themselves into a womanly figure after a time. Acne, though still relentless, eventually began to silence its flames to uncover a not-so-bad-looking face.

When I consider the stages of life, I often think of them in segments that correlate to age. The first is what I call *The Stage of Learning*. This typically takes place in our 20s and 30s and is a time of dreams and discovery. This learning period helps shape who we are and forge the imaginings we have for ourselves and our lives. It is the time when we begin the process of unearthing who we want to be.

In this stage, we encounter acceptance and adjustment as we start to come to grips with the fact that some of our ideas, ideals, and visions may require some modification. Yet, we are still brave and fearless enough to embrace the fine-tuning needed to become the woman of our dreams. This is the phase of life when we are still learning who we are, what we want, and how to best achieve it all. But it is just that, a stage. One that we will soon grow out of as we enter *The Stage of Living*.

The Stage of Living is the period of our 40s and 50s and is a time of direction and determination. I often think of the song that the great Chaka Khan made into the classic anthem, *I'm Every Woman*. This stage is when we believe that we can have it all, do it all, and be all. We are generally focused on family and career during this period, living life in both the boardroom and the bedroom with a fierce determination that we can handle it all.

I often think of this as the time of life when it is all about advancement and authenticity. It is that period when we are climbing the corporate ladder and growing to be less concerned with what others think about us than what we feel about ourselves. We have navigated the growth of our children and the maturing of our relationships. This is when our focus becomes more about being the woman we want to be than the woman everyone else thinks we should be. We are equipped to deal with the fact that all of our dreams from the former stage may not come true while being strong enough to dream new dreams.

This is the period when we must learn to place value on our own needs, as so much of our time has been invested in the lives of others. We are living life to the fullest while knowing that we are on the precipice of something that will bring about a significant change. At the same time, we are still strong enough to face the days ahead and prepare to take the next hill with gusto.

The third stage is *The Stage of Legacy*. This is the period of life from our 60s and beyond. I often think of this as a time of deliberation and decisiveness. During this phase, we realize we have already lived longer than we will. We begin to assess our lives through planning and making proper decisions. I believe this is when we get sharper. We recognize that our most valuable assets are not the things we accumulated in the previous stages. We realize they are in the abundance of wisdom, insight, and vision afforded us throughout our lives. Instead of upgrading, we desire to downsize. We discover that less is more, and more is measured in moments and contentment instead of additional acquisitions.

This is also the time of adaptation and allocation. We must now adjust to this new version of ourselves. This stage requires some revisioning, as our bodies are often what sometimes seems like light-years older than our minds. (I cannot tell you the number of times I have to stop to figure out why my physical person does not execute all the instructions given by the mental version of myself.) This stage also requires a reallocation of time. I like to say that we can do everything we always did. It just takes a bit longer to recover.

Regardless of what the stages of life bring and irrespective of their duration, a stage is nothing more than a period that we will grow out of or move through eventually. It is also one to which we will probably never return. Despite the joys and challenges and ups and downs, these stages are by no means the same as our lives' seasons.

Like the natural seasons, the seasons of life are specific, cyclical, and bring with them opportunities that must be seized within the period of their appearance. The English evangelist and author Leonard Ravenhill is believed to have originated the quote, "The opportunity of a lifetime must be seized within the lifetime of the opportunity." What a perfect depiction of the importance of being able to distinguish those seasons from mere stages. To understand my point more adequately, let us uncover the words of one who has been labeled as the wisest man ever to live.

In one of the most popular and regularly quoted biblical passages, King Solomon penned these words: *"To everything there is a season, a time for every purpose under heaven."*[2] In this passage, the word translated *season* is from the Hebrew word *zeman*, meaning an appointed occasion.[3] Its primitive root, *zaman*, means to fix a time or to appoint.[4] The wise King Solomon goes on to say that there is a time for every purpose. The word translated time speaks of desire, a valuable thing or matter, as something in mind.[5]

When we consider the original meanings, it appears that the great King Solomon was explaining that life is comprised of seasons, and within every season, there is a precise timeframe that is most conducive to accomplishing a specific and valuable objective. Simply said, within every season, there is a now moment to achieve a useful purpose.

I like to think of the seasons of our lives as prime time, those points in life that are bursting with exact times to accomplish great exploits. As such, we must exercise caution to ensure that we are not ascribing excessive time and intention to something that may be nothing more than a stage.

One morning I awoke with the line from an old soap opera ringing in my head: "Like sands through the hourglass, these are the days of our lives." Almost immediately, I sensed the voice of the Lord saying, "The thing is, I do not measure your minutes. I measure your moments." That one statement helped solidify my understanding. Regardless of what stage of life we find ourselves in, we must discover those "now moments" that have been opened to produce valuable purpose within the opportune time we have been given.

Season Thoughts

❖ Think about some of the stages you have experienced in life and how they impacted you. In what ways might you have mislabeled a stage of life thinking of it as a season?

❖ In which of the life stages are you currently: the stage of learning, living, or legacy?

❖ How do you see those stages differing from the seasons of life?

❖ What is your understanding of the difference between a stage and a season? How does that impact your thinking about where you are in your own life?

Chapter Two:
Every Season Has Its Fruit

Everything does not grow in every season. The first Psalm opens with a clear statement. It speaks of the blessedness that is promised to those who choose to delight themselves in the precepts and statutes of the Lord. Describing what that person will be like, the beginning of verse three says, *"He shall be like a tree planted by the rivers of water, that brings forth its fruit in its season."*

There is no need for extraordinary exegetical skills here. Just as a student of the obvious, the word picture makes clear what we already know. Every tree has its own fruit, and every fruit has its own season of production.

You might ask, why make such a distinction about what is so apparent? My answer would be two-fold. The first reason I bring this to light is that we must realize that, like individual trees, there is a specific fruit that grows from each of our lives.

The psalmist tells us that the planted tree brings forth "its fruit." Too often, we miss the grace and beauty of what is being produced in our lives. We become distracted by looking at, longing after, or becoming envious of what is being birthed from someone else's life.

With the boundless and broad reach of social media, we now experience 24/7 coverage of the activities of others' lives. We live with a constant stream of the events of real and cyber friends. While it is wonderful to have an opportunity to celebrate the accomplishments of others, too often, we fall prey to comparison. This causes us to miss recognizing what is special and unique that is to be delivered through us. Without intending to, we end up violating scriptural admonitions and limiting our importance and effectiveness based upon what we believe others may have to offer.

Even when we share the same gifts and graces, fruit from the tree of our life will possess the uniqueness of who we have been made to be. That fruit can only be developed as we grasp and appreciate the masterful design of our individuality. Such realization is essential for, as Beth Moore put it, "God is busy making you someone no one else has ever been."[6]

The second reason for distinguishing what may already be apparent is this. Even though everything will not grow from our lives within every season, there is no season in our life when we cannot be productive. I learned this lesson several years ago through a casual conversation. It has continued to influence me as I have moved through various seasons of my life.

For a long time, my family and I lived in a home situated on two acres of land. As the years progressed, we became more and more concerned that the towering pine trees on the property would snap during the icy Georgia winters and potentially damage our home. So, we secured our landscaper's services and had the entire parcel completely cleared and new landscaping designed and installed.

One day as I checked on the plantings' progress, I expressed my disappointment that we did not undertake the project earlier in the year.

Realizing that the fall season was coming swiftly to a close, I said to him, "I wish we had done this earlier in the year so that I could enjoy the beauty of what you are planting."

Much to my surprise, our landscaper responded, "Oh, you do not have to worry about that. I am planting things that are designed to grow in every season."[7]

Although winter was rapidly approaching, he could plant for the impending season because of his knowledge. When winter came, there was interestingly beautiful foliage at our home because it was designed for that season. And although it could not be sustained with the warmth of the following spring that came around, that did not affect our home's curb appeal. By then, something else was growing in its place.

The great truth is that there is something in your season that you can gain, but there is also something in your season that you can grow! Suppose a landscape artist's skill and wisdom can produce extraordinary beauty for each season. How much more has God filled our lives with fruit that will best display His grace and effectively bring nourishment to those who need to eat from our tree in every season?

Look for the fruit that has been designed to grow in your season. Not only is it present, but it is necessary to display the Master Designer's handiwork.

Season Thoughts

❖ Read Psalm 1:1-3 and Matthew 24:32. What insights do you gain from these passages concerning fruitfulness?

❖ What are some special and unique graces of your life that you have overlooked by comparing yourself to others?

❖ What was one of the more challenging seasons of your life? What did you gain from that season? What are you now able to give as a result of going through that season?

❖ What was one of the most precious seasons of your life? What did you gain from that season? What are you now able to give as a result of going through that season?

Chapter Three:
God Controls the Seasons

You may not be able to identify with this, but I like to control certain aspects of my life. I am not exactly a Type A personality, but I am a planner, and, as such, I prefer a life that squares with my list.

I am a fan of the old-time management courses that taught you to spend the last thirty minutes of your workday preparing a list of the next day's tasks. I must admit to the deep sense of satisfaction that comes from seeing yellow highlighter across the lines of that list. Regrettably, that sense of accomplishment can sometimes be challenged when the yellow on my list pales in the light of what seems to be a day of endless interruptions and unplanned items.

But as much as I want to exercise the direction of my day and regulate the outcomes of my efforts, my heart knows that I am not in control of anything. Am I suggesting that plans should not be made? Absolutely not! I do not think I could survive in a world where every day is a venture in flying by the proverbial seat of my pants. However, I recognize that despite all of our plans, it is God's purpose that must always be the ultimate target of the outcome.[8] And such it is with the seasons of our lives.

When we read the book of Daniel, we meet King Nebuchadnezzar, a powerful ruler. He finds himself confounded by a dream that has rendered him sleepless. No one in his employ can interpret the dream. This makes the king so enraged that he determines to kill all the magicians, astrologers, sorcerers, and others responsible for deciphering such things. Their inability to convey the dream and deliver its interpretation resulted in the start of a plan to destroy all Babylon's wise men. But God had strategically placed a gifted young man who, in his humility, was able to recognize the greatness of the One he served.

When made aware of the impending execution of all the wise men of Babylon, Daniel enlisted the help of his companions. He sought the Lord with these words: *"Blessed be the name of God forever and ever, for wisdom and might are His. And He changes the times and the seasons..."9*

Clearly, Daniel was not talking about seasons in terms of weather since he went on to talk about God elevating and lowering kings. Daniel was conveying to the king that everything that happens in life, whether one chooses to acknowledge it or not, is because of God's greatness. Daniel recognized God as the Master Architect whose authority exceeded that of any natural king. He was confident that God held the seasons of life in His grip. Daniel knew that God could be trusted to render the appropriate answer for the conditions under which he and his friends were found.

Another passage that helps us embrace the concept of God's control of seasons is in the first chapter of the book of Acts. In his account to Theophilus, the physician Luke details Christ's interaction with His disciples during the forty days following His resurrection. As they assembled, the first question they posed to Jesus centered around whether He would restore the kingdom to Israel. It is in verse seven that we find Jesus' response to their question.

He said, *"It is not for you to know times or seasons which the Father has put in His own authority."*

I am of the mind that words were never arbitrarily dropped into the ancient text. As such, it is essential to note that Jesus uses two distinctly different words to denote portions of time.

He said it was not for them to know *times*, which in Greek is *chronos*. This word signifies the quantity or extent of time. Much like the meaning of the English word chronology, this speaks of a sequential form of time arranged in dates, periods, and events. It is the time that we measure in minutes and by which we are bound in this sphere.

However, and most important to the point, He did not limit His use of terminology to *chronos* time. Instead, He added that it was not for His disciples to know the *seasons* that God has mandated to His authority. The Greek word for *seasons* is *kairos* which, unlike measurable time, speaks of occasions and set times.

Listen to Acts 1:7 in a few transliterations:

And he said to them, "It is not for you to have knowledge of the time and the order of events which the Father has kept in his control." – Bible in Basic English

Jesus said to them, "The times and occasions are set by my Father's own authority, and it is not for you to know when they will be." – Today's English Version

He said to them, "It is not yours to know the chronological events in the passing of time nor the strategic, epochal periods of time

which the Father placed within the sphere of His own private authority." – Wuest Expanded New Testament.

Many years ago, I heard the late Dr. Myles Munroe speak about seasons. During that time, he made a statement that profoundly impacted my thinking from that point forward. He said, "You cannot control a season, and you cannot change a season. All you can do is cooperate with a season." Since then, I have thought of many amusing illustrations of that truth. Here is one for your consideration.

Imagine yourself standing in the dead of winter clad only in a bathing suit as blustering winds and harsh elements beat upon your exposed body. The reality is that no amount of confessing, rebuking, or defiance will change the winter season elements you are experiencing. If you are smart, you will quickly accept your best option. You will concede that you are not in control and promptly exercise wisdom to change into attire that is better suited for the period.

Most of our struggles come when we spend more time trying to change a season rather than seeking to be prepared by the One who controls it. Sheila Walsh said it best when she wrote that our impatience to have God move now, to act in ways that make sense to us, will drive us to take control of our lives.[10] The most effective and beneficial approach is to yield to God's authority. We must trust His love and seek to determine what we should be learning, doing, and giving while in each season of life.

It is vital to remember that, because God is in control of our lives' seasons, we must be careful to avoid cursing what He has designed to help us grow. Instead, we should anticipate that something good will come from the season if for no other reason than the One who is in control has our best interest at heart.

Season Thoughts

❖ How does the thought of not being in control affect you?

❖ What do you think are some of the reasons it is so difficult to release control of our lives to God?

❖ In Giving God Your Future, Sheila Walsh is quoted as saying, "God is moving in ways that we cannot see or understand. This means we are left with the question, 'Do I trust Him?'" In what areas have you personally found it most challenging to relinquish control to God?

❖ In your own words, describe the difference between chronos and kairos. List some examples from your life that would fall into each category?

❖ Read Romans 8:28, Ephesians 1:11, Ephesians 3:11, and 2 Timothy 1:9. Although the Bible does not use the word "control," how do these passages speak to you about God's control of our lives?

❖ When have you found yourself complaining about or "cursing" what God was doing in your life? Write out your confession of that time, followed by a prayer of repentance.

Chapter Four:
Sowing and Reaping

Whether or not you have ever stepped foot into a church or onto a farm, you probably have heard the phrase, "you reap what you sow." Most of the time, the term is used as a reminder of the punitive recourse one can expect as a result of doing something wrong. But that is only a narrow view of a broader truth. If you will indulge me for a moment, I would like to look at sowing and reaping as more of an agricultural phenomenon and less of a biblical indictment. This way, we can glean some valuable insight relative to the seasons of life.

The first and obvious thing to recognize is that we indeed reap *what* we sow. Although what the farmer plants look significantly different than what will be harvested, he can only expect to receive a crop of the same genetic makeup as that which was planted. Anyone planting apple seeds would in no way be expecting the production of anything other than apple trees. Despite the many factors that impact growth, time of planting, soil conditions, sufficient sunlight, and rain, nothing changes the expected outcome. The seed that is sown determines the harvest that will be reaped.

Another vital truth of sowing and reaping is that we reap *more than* what we sow. Despite growing up in a city, I learned this lesson from my Southern-born grandparents, who migrated to the north. I suppose you might say that they fit the old adage that says you can take the person out of the country, but you cannot take the country out of the person. Although we lived in a single-family home in Brooklyn, that did not stop my maternal grandfather from deciding to plant corn around the perimeter of our small backyard.

I do not recall the time or the process when he actually planted. Still, I became well acquainted with the results of his labor. All around our urban garden were stalks as tall as my ten-year-old frame, each of which held multiple ears of corn.

What my grandfather planted was immeasurably less than what we gained, and what we harvested reproduced itself season after season. While he may not have known the extent of his plantings, he understood one thing. He could expect that the ground in our tiny backyard was guaranteed to yield far more than what it had been given. As a result, he would reap more than what he sowed.

Beyond reaping what we sow and more than we sow is the equally profound yet straightforward insight that we can only reap *after* we sow. As a part of God's covenant with creation after the flood, He promised that as long as the earth continued, there would be seedtime and harvest.[11] Considering the natural process of cultivation, I am confident that we can also render the promise that there will be seed, followed by time, and then harvest. After all, nothing grows instantaneously. There is always a time lapse between seed and crop, between planting and harvesting, and between sowing and reaping. While we do not determine the time, we can be confident that there will be a lapse of time after we sow, followed by a harvest.

By now, you may be wondering, why has she spent so much time on this issue of sowing and reaping? In addition to the fact that we reap what we sow, more than we sow, and after we sow, it is also true that we reap only *if* we sow. What we sow in one season of life will determine the kind and abundance of what we reap in the next. Conversely, if we do not put anything in the ground of our lives in one season, we will be void of a harvest in the next.

Sometimes the challenges and difficulties of a season threaten to hinder our energy and cause us to spend more time complaining than contemplating. It is in those times that we run the risk of being like the person described in the proverb that says, *"The lazy man will not plow because of winter; He will beg during harvest and have nothing."*[12]

We must always guard against falling prey to becoming so entrenched in our current situation that we fail to find the parcel awaiting a seed. When things are hard, we must build up the endurance to find the best plot. We must dig up the fallow ground and purposefully allow the Lord to plant something in our hearts that will burst into a fruitful vine in the future. Conditions are rarely perfect, but imperfect conditions do not have to stop the sowing process.

Regardless of the season in which you find yourself, know that there is a seed waiting. When placed deep within the soil of your heart, that seed will germinate and develop into something that will propel you further in your next season. It may even grow enough to sustain you and those who are blessed to eat from your garden.

Season Thoughts

❖ When you have heard the phrase, you reap what you sow, have you processed it as more punitive or positive? Explain why.

❖ How do you interpret the idea of reaping what you sow, more than you sow, after you sow, and if you sow? What are some examples of how any or all of these have manifested in your life?

❖ During this season of your life, which have you been doing more of, complaining or contemplating? How can you do less of the former and more of the latter?

❖ What can you plant in this season that will provide a return on your life in the next?

❖ Read Ecclesiastes 11:4 in at least three translations. Afterward, write in your own words the insight you gain from the passage.

Chapter Five:
Miss the Season, Miss the Fruit

Here is the point for your consideration, plain and simple. *If you do not recognize a season, you will lose time and miss the purpose.* There is a now moment for every purpose, every desire, every matter, and everything important. In other words, within a season, you have a purpose, but there is only a time to get it done. You and I cannot afford to miss the seasons within our lives because we ultimately miss the purpose that the season was intended to yield if we do.

Have you ever done something and then thought it was like you were in just the right place at the right time? The reality is that if you were in the right place a few minutes earlier or later, you would have missed the time and had no idea about the purpose that was to be accomplished. You thought you were getting a deal and did not realize that God was dealing with your life. Dare I even say, dealing with your destiny. I can honestly say that my life is replete with those "now moments." I can look back and say if I missed that season, I would have missed significant destiny and fruitfulness for myself and others.

One such time that comes to my mind was when I moved to Georgia in 1985. One of my best girlfriends had already moved to Atlanta a few months before and had been checking out churches for my upcoming move. On the first Sunday in January of 1986, she announced, "I know exactly where we are going to church today." I agreed with her and was surprised when I almost immediately felt a sense of connection to the place. I would like to say that I quickly and obediently followed the inner prompting to make that place my church home. But sadly, I must confess that I rationalized myself right out of the opportunity with all-too-appropriate excuses.

"This is not like my church in New York."

"If this is the place for me, then my friend should be joining too. After all, I do not know anyone else in this city."

"Perhaps I need to check them out for a few more Sundays to see if this is really the place for me."

I left the service with the sad feeling that I had just talked myself out of something important. Before I could exit the parking lot, I made an internal promise that I would come back the next week and be obedient to the step I needed to take for this new season of my life. The following week I made good on that inner commitment and joined the church that I had visited only one week before.

Now I can already hear you asking the question, what did your decision to join a church after one visit have to do with seasons and fruit? I am more than happy to tell you the answer. You see, little did I know that the purpose of my becoming a part of that church was beyond a worship location. I later discovered that the man who was to become my husband had experienced a similarly strange draw to that church just six months prior. After becoming friends and partners in the music ministry, we became husband and wife.

You see, the purpose within that season was not merely to get me to the right church. It was to get me to the right person. Had I missed the moment within the season, I would have lost the fruit of more than three decades of a fulfilling and impactful marriage. As I consider that much of what I am doing in life and ministry has been primarily due to this godly man's encouragement, I can see that even more fruit has abounded to my account than just what is a part of our relationship. Some of that fruit is being enjoyed by those whose lives I have touched in some way.

Referred to as the dean of American preaching, the late Rev. Dr. Gardner C. Taylor was quoted as saying, "There are seasons and eras, and we have to see what they are as best we can and find what is positive in them."[13] Every season of life will not look or feel productive, but it is critical to recognize that there is something of high value that comes out of each. It is up to us to be diligent in every season, seeking to be obedient in the now moments so that we do not lose time and miss the purpose.

Dr. Daryl R. Van Tongeren wrote, "Life seems to operate in seasons. Some parts of life are like spring: new beginnings, a fresh start, a brand-new job, or a creative opportunity. Starting things always feels so exciting, so invigorating, and so hopeful. The possibilities are endless. Summer is when living seems easier. Just like in life, sometimes things just click. Relationships are thriving, work seems effortless, and the pleasant days are long. Autumn brings a cool, refreshing change, but always a twinge of nostalgia of days lost and the foreboding reminder of what lies away. Life sometimes changes, which makes us remember (and long for) the past; we leave friends for a new chapter, say goodbye to a loved one, or move for another opportunity. And then, as certain as ever, winter arrives. The cold, bitter harshness of a season that indiscriminately tests the mettle of us all. It begs the question: how strong are you?"[14]

When we look at the natural seasons, we find some elements or characteristics that parallel with where we sometimes find ourselves emotionally and spiritually. Taking a look at these correlations will help us understand what we need to be doing in those seasons of life. Therefore, let us journey into these natural seasons to identify where we may currently be and how best to grow within that period.

Season Thoughts

❖ Name a time when you think you missed an opportune moment. What fruit did you miss as a result?

❖ Name a time when you found yourself in the right place at the right time. What prompted you to take advantage of that moment?

❖ How have you seen a "now moment" work in your favor? How has your moment worked for the benefit of someone else?

❖ Consider a time that did not seem productive but ended up yielding great value. What purpose would you have missed had you not recognized the value of the moment, even though it was difficult?

Chapter Six:
Dark Nights of the Soul

L odged between fall and spring, winter is by far the coldest season of the year. Depending on where you reside, this season brings long nights, short days, plunging temperatures, chilling dampness, and biting frost. But as depressing as that may sound, winter's actual job is to create conditions and advantages that prepare the earth for beauty on the horizon.

In Genesis 8:22, we are first introduced to the word winter as a natural and recurring season. *"While the earth remains, seedtime and harvest, cold and heat, winter and summer, and day and night shall not cease."* In this passage, the Hebrew word for winter is *charaph*, which means to pull off or, by implication, to expose by stripping.[15]

I am sure you would agree that we generally do not associate images of pulling off or exposing when we think of the winter season. Instead, we see it as a time of secluding and layering. From a natural standpoint, to remain warm during the colder climate, we put on more and more. For some of us, winter finds us layering ourselves with clothing. We comfort ourselves with foods and avoid activities that will remove us from the nest of coziness we have created in our homes. Then when the season ends, we are shocked by what we find lurking under the layers.

Similarly, we experience winter seasons of life when we seem to go through what St. John of the Cross referred to as dark nights of the soul. The blustery winds of a winter season of the soul might come in a myriad of ways. It could be through a marriage that ends due to death or one hit by the fatal blow of disloyalty. Maybe it is having to watch children compromise their youth while an aging loved one bargains for more time. It could be observing once-dark curls yield to snowy gray tresses long before we have had an opportunity to fulfill all our dreams. Regardless of the cause, life's winters can appear cold, barren, and nonproductive. We want to pull away emotionally, desperately reaching for anything that will provide a semblance of comfort or cover. But I would like to suggest a different approach to the winters of life.

When we find ourselves in a personal winter, it is actually the season for inventory, not hiding. This time of dormancy provides the best opportunities for inspection, pruning, and identifying the defects that may have lodged in the root system of our heart. This is not the time to rely on our feelings, as they may be faulty at best. While walking through a dark season, if we attempt to navigate our lives by what we feel, we will run aground onto the rocks. We must navigate by what we know is true no matter what we feel.[16]

Taking personal inventory is not easy. Preferring to stay within the grips of rigidity and hardness as opposed to self-reflection is commonplace. The natural tendency is to withdraw, giving way to feelings of isolation. We may even find it hard to rejoice with others whom we see blooming all around us. But, even more than any other time, this is when we must ward off comparison and focus our attention on God's purposes. It is in the winter season of life that we must ask the critical questions of Him:

What do you want me to gain during this time?

What are the lessons you want me to learn now?

How do you want me to dig further down and gain deeper roots?

There is an enemy of your soul, and he would like nothing more than for you to become depressed because of the shortage of visible fruit. That is why it is vital to understand the purpose of life's winter seasons. Winter is the time when what is most important is not what is above the ground but what is germinating deep in the recesses of one's soul. What lies below is not dead. It is deepening. If you focus on what is above the ground, you will risk improperly stewarding the seed that will grow and blossom later on in life.

The truth of the matter is that we simply cannot produce visible fruit all of the time. At some point, we must have a period of rest.

In the Old Testament, God demonstrated the sabbath's importance by insisting upon a year of rest for the land. Listen to the instructions given in Leviticus 25:1-4:

And the Lord spoke to Moses on Mount Sinai, saying, "Speak to the children of Israel, and say to them: When you come into the land which I give you, then the land shall keep a sabbath to the Lord. Six years you shall sow your field, and six years you shall prune your vineyard and gather its fruit; but in the seventh year, there shall be a sabbath of solemn rest for the land, a sabbath to the Lord. You shall neither sow your field nor prune your vineyard."

While Moses was on Mount Sinai, the Lord gave him these instructions for the people of Israel. "When you come into the land I am going to give you, you must let the land rest before the Lord every seventh year. For six years you may sow your field and prune your vineyards and harvest your crops, but during the seventh year the land is to lie fallow before the lord, uncultivated. Do not sow your crops and don't prune your vineyards during that entire year."
– The Living Bible

The Hebrew word for *sabbath* means to repose and desist from exertion. It is an intermission intended to allow time for restoration and rejuvenation. Even our physical being requires a time of repose. In the words of Beth Moore, "Beloved, I am convinced one of our severest needs is pure rest. Not only sleep, but refreshment and recreation."[17]

Each time I look at the crepe myrtles in my yard, I am reminded of the importance of the winter seasons of my life. During winter, these trees are absolutely bare and unattractive. They appear as though they are dead, with no promise of a beautiful future. But, as you know, they are far from lifeless. They have simply undergone the pruning process that gives them the ability to manufacture nourishment in the trunk to produce in their next season.

In the same way, the winter season of your life does not mean that you are done, that you are lost, or that nothing is happening. Winter is the time for inside work. It is the season to deal with your private life. If you intend to grow anything in the next season, you will have to spend more time in prayer and the Word. What you are cultivating and growing internally requires a current Selah.

If you find yourself in a winter season of life, be encouraged and determined to see it for what it is intended. The winters of life are times of pause and solemn rest, times when there is sufficient growth to live on while more is being developed quietly. Patsy Clairmont said it like this: "Life is treacherous, and life is tremendous. We all know this, but here is the clincher. The stabilizing truth that acts as a cohesive to hold us together is that, through all life's weather patterns, God is good."[18]

As I write this chapter, I am reminded of a lesson that I learned from my window. I stood at the sink, vigorously washing the last of the dishes. In the process, my eyes fixed upon the beauty of the lake behind my house. This view is one of the features that make this my dream home. Nothing calms and centers me like being in my home and, even though we were in the winter season, the landscape still brought me great peace. The zoysia grass had grown dormant and was casting a yellowish-green hue. The deciduous trees had long lost their leaves, yet they stood stately and without embarrassment despite being unclothed.

This was not a new vista for me as we had lived in this center of tranquility for more than eleven years at the time. So what made me pause and give attention to the wonders of winter? It was when I shifted my eyes to the right and looked out of the large eleven-foot windows of the keeping room. (Why do they call it a "keeping room" anyway?) Through that new look, I gained a perspective I had not noticed in all the previous years.

Thanks to yielding to this new and seemingly barren season, the trees that would typically serve as a visual buffer between our property and our neighbors were now bare.

Their newfound nakedness opened their arms to reveal shimmering ripples as the cold breeze carried the sun-drenched water across the lake. Suddenly it dawned on me that, like this moment, the winter seasons of our lives seem to strip us of so much, often leaving us feeling vulnerable and emotionally undressed. But if we would look in a new direction, we would find that what the season actually did was broaden the way to a new view of beauty that was there all along—perhaps just overlooked because of the showiness of a better and brighter season.

I finished my chores at the sink with a new conviction. When I arrive in another winter season, I am determined to take an intentional look to find the great treasures that may have been overlooked. Winter is not necessarily bleak, barren, or bad. If you stand tall and unashamed of the things that have dropped off your life, you may just find a breathtaking woman who is full of deep and resonating displays of beauty and grandeur.

Like the natural season, the winters of life can teach us much about mindfulness and the gift of the present.[19] In the same way, the winter season of life can and should be a time when we recognize that what may look like dormancy is nothing more than a pause or a "selah." It is an opportunity to stop, breathe, dig down, reflect, and prepare to move into the next season of life with gratitude and greater fortitude.

Think about it. Winter brings the blessing of Christmas, the celebrations of a new year, and the beauty of snow. Although winter is not full of bright colors, who can deny the magic and originality of snowflakes?

Season Thoughts

❖ Read Psalm 16:7, Galatians 6:9, and 1 Peter 1:6-8. What insight do you gain from these passages as it relates to living through what St. John of the Cross referred to as dark nights of the soul?

❖ After reading The Winters of Life, consider some life circumstances that may lead to a winter season (e.g., death, divorce, challenges with children, caregiving, unfulfilled dreams, etc.). How have any of these, or others, impacted you personally?

❖ If you are in the winter season now, which of the responses have you noticed in your life? Rigidity? Withdrawal? Isolation?

❖ Now, take some time to consider the following four ways to use the winter season for your benefit. For each one, write out what that would look like for you and how you believe you can employ its benefit in this season:

  ➤ *Inventory*: taking time for self-reflection.
  ➤ *Inspection*: discovering God's purpose.
  ➤ *Intermission*: practicing restoration and rejuvenation.
  ➤ *Intentionality*: becoming mindful of the treasures within and around you.

❖ If you are not currently in the winter season, how might you use this information to assist someone else?

Chapter Seven:
Here Comes the Sun

No one can turn a phrase like King Solomon. Who knows, that might be why he could attract three hundred wives and seven hundred concubines. Though not the focus of his sonnet, in chapter two of the Song of Solomon, the king paints what I find to be one of the most beautiful word pictures for the introduction of the spring season. *"For behold, the winter is past; the rain is over and gone. The flowers appear on the earth, the time of singing has come, and the voice of the turtledove is heard in our land. The fig tree ripens its figs, and the vines are in blossom; they give forth fragrance."*[20]

The first day of spring is called the Vernal Equinox. From Latin, *vernal* means spring, and *equinox* means equal days. On the first day of spring, the sunrise and the sunset are about twelve hours apart everywhere on the earth, making the hours of daylight and night almost equal. This is the time of year when days get longer and warmer, and it is hailed as the season of new beginnings. Spring transitions us from the barrenness of winter to the warmth of new days.

And who does not enjoy warmth, beauty, and newness of life? Although our Gregorian calendar is the most widely used in the world, introducing the year in the winter season, the Bible positions spring as the season of beginnings. Second Samuel 11:1 (KJV) refers to it as coming *after the year was expired*. Second Kings 13:20 (KJV) hails it *at the coming of the year* and specifically names *Abib*[21] as the first month for the Israelites. At that time, the Passover was instituted. The Israelites left Egypt, the Tabernacle was set up, and Israel crossed the Jordan. And if those were not significant enough for you, it is the season that Jesus died and was resurrected. You just cannot get any more "new beginning" than that!

Just as spring calls us back to nature, fills our sails with warmer winds, soothes our weary bones, and lifts our spirits[22], so the spring season of life fills us with anticipation of the coming alive of everything—the beginning of all things exciting and fresh. We shed what has imprisoned us and embrace our freedom with an eye toward newness and goodness. What has been planted in previous seasons begins to show itself, even if only in bud form.

This is the season when we view life through fresh eyes of vibrancy, favor, and blessing. We feel as though we can inhale deeply and revel in the breeze of grace that seems to gently wash away the layers of the shorter, darker, and colder times we have transitioned from in life. We approach the spring of life with a renewed sense of hope. While appreciating the victory of having pushed through more challenging times, we stand in a place of greater expectation for what is yet ahead.

The spring season of life is the time to enjoy the wonders of new life. It is when we can bask in the beauty of what God is doing in and around us. This is the time for expressing gratitude for the peace and calm that has been ushered in. Now is not time to be guilty about the blessings of the Lord. There is nothing wrong with soaking in the warmth and feeling your shoulders drop as the weights of life are lifted. Take it all in and savor the moments this period provides.

In the natural spring season, for the earth to allow new life to burst forth, it must accept the saturation that comes from the rain. In like manner, when we live in our spring season, we cannot forget that there will be some damp days and maybe even some storms to produce continued growth. We must understand that the elements present within the season are designed to keep softening the earth of our hearts. This saturation is not to be seen as something bleak but rather as a refreshing that will enable us to blossom to a greater degree than we already are.

During the occasional rainy days and stormy nights, we must resist the temptation to complain about their arrival. Those days are not designed to minimize our joy. Instead, they are the days when we are privileged to be cleansed by the clearing away of pollutants from previous times of challenge that may be lingering in our heart unaware. As Warren Wiersbe puts it, "The same sun that brings beauty out of the seeds also exposes the vermin hiding under the rocks."[23]

Just as the combination of earth's rain and the sun produces the beauty of rainbows, the meshing of life's rain with the light of the Son will garner more extraordinary beauty in the life of the one walking in the spring season of life. As a precious sister in the Lord once told me, "Not all storms come to disrupt our lives. Some storms may come to clear new paths."[24]

As is the case with every season, there are pitfalls we must be on the lookout for too. So while we are enjoying the wonders, delights, and peace of the season, we must not fall prey to emotional or spiritual "spring fever" or "spring break." This is not the time to skip out on the school of life or stroll aimlessly through the days. The spring season of life is when we can be lulled into ineffectiveness, spending more time daydreaming than being watchful. Our minds can drift into endless hours of inactivity, creating a false sense that things will always be bright and beautiful.

We must resist the urge to throw off all restraint while stopping to smell the roses. We must be vigilant, not becoming intoxicated by the season to the point that we either become puffed up in displaying our blessings or drifting off into complacency, as though things will remain the same forever. Do not misunderstand me. The spring season of life is a wonderful time to exhale, relax, and recharge. But we must recognize that, as with every season, this one has a purpose as well. Remember that this is the season for planting, not showing off. It is also the time when there will be some pruning for a later and more abundant harvest.

Some say that we most enjoy the season in which we are born. If that is true, then having an April birthday may explain my love for spring. I delight in leaving the cold of winter for warmer days and, if I am completely transparent, I sometimes wish that I could stay in that season of excitement, new beginnings, anticipation, hope, and a fresh new start. Similarly, we love the spring season of life when everything is blooming for us, and, understandably, we would want to stay in that place forever—or at least as long as possible. After all, who would not want to live perpetually in a life of flowers, singing, ripening trees, and blossoming fragrant vines, right? But we all know that seasons do not last forever.

If I asked you what the names Benson, Crawford, Jones, Simone, Streisand, and Wilson have in common, depending on your stage of life, you might guess that they are all noted musicians and singers from a few decades ago. But what you may not realize is something else that they all have in common. At some point in their careers, they all recorded a song entitled "Everything Must Change," originally written by jazz musician and songwriter Benard Ighner. Besides being one of my all-time favorite songs, the lyrics are a beautiful reminder of the ever-changing seasons of every person's life.

Everything must change
Nothing stays the same
Everyone must change
Nothing stays the same

The young become the old
Mysteries do unfold
Cause that's the way of time
Nothing and no one goes unchanged

Winter turns to spring
A wounded heart will heal
But never much too soon
Everything must change

The young become the old
Mysteries do unfold

Cause that's the way of time
Nothing and no one goes unchanged

There are not many things in life
You can be sure of
Except rain comes from the clouds
And sun lights up the sky
And hummingbirds do fly

Precious one, enjoy the spring of your life thoroughly, use the time well, and get everything God intended for you before the season changes. Appreciate what is growing, even though it may only be a bud at the moment. And when you feel that season begin to change, be determined to pass to another with grace and strength, recognizing that wherever you land next, God is already there with a purpose for you to fulfill.

Season Thoughts

❖ What have been the most memorable spring seasons of life for you?

❖ If you are currently in the spring season of your life, what are some of the new things God is trying to bring to you? What are some of the things that God is trying to bring out of you?

❖ With every beautiful spring comes rainy days and stormy nights. How have you been processing those times?

❖ What are some issues from a previous season that may be hindering you from fully giving birth to something new in this season?

❖ If you are not currently in the spring season of life, how are you relating to other women who are enjoying springtime now?

Chapter Eight:
The Heat Is On

Following the newness of spring and foreshadowing the cool of autumn lies the heat of summer. Our entire biological system is linked to the sun's rising and setting, and our circadian rhythms begin to dance as we experience more sunlight and rising temperatures each day. This is the time of year when everything in us yearns for the outdoors.

We love summer because school is out, responsibilities are lifted, and vacation is on the horizon. We cannot wait to shed our clothes and discard our cares. With face toward the sun, we close our eyes and drink in the warmth of the long days, and with little concern for time, we gladly embrace the stillness of short, muggy nights.

In 1935, a cast of classically trained African American singers performed in an opera entitled Porgy and Bess. After more than eighty years and countless renditions, one of the most iconic songs from that production continues to be *Summertime*. More than 85 years after the opera's debut, multiple generations and artists from varying genres keep the song alive as they open their performance with the words, *Summertime, and the living is easy...*" And that is how we feel in the summer season of life.

This is the season that finds us shaking off the cares that have been weighing on our shoulders and preparing ourselves for a time of rest and reprieve. We are comfortable allowing our minds to vacate for a while, not so much in idleness as in renewal. It is the season of the deepest exhale.

The summer of life is also a time of visible growth and maturity. What began flowering in the springtime of life is now in full bloom—vibrant, evident, and discernable by all who get to watch us walk through the season. This growth enables us to weather the occasional thunderstorm with grace because we recognize that the showers do not last long. More than anything, life's momentary rains are perceived as a relief from the consistent and blistering heat of the good times.

Without a doubt, there is a measure of rest in the summer season that we do and should enjoy. We are allowed to pull back from the challenges of other seasons and resign from past woes. Depending upon our individual personalities, we may need a moment to sink into the guilt-free rest that the season affords. But even the most hardworking of us learn to quickly acquiesce to the rhythm of a time out when needed. The spiritual and emotional commitment to discipline and initiative of previous seasons lands us in the lush fields of the summer season when we have little need to toil.

Indeed, living is easy during this season, as we are now prepared to live off of what already exists. Like the wise ants of the Proverbs, we have stored up the lessons of past seasons—both good and bad, both painless and tough. We are now prepared to lift our sails and coast in the tranquility of accessible waters. Summer sisters understand that the ride is pleasant, not because of any unique gifting or ability of their own, but simply because the Captain of the sea is faithful to navigate the journey.

The summer seasons of life deliver uplifted moods and supercharged energy. This is the time when we are ready to release negativity and strengthen relationships. To borrow a thought from Luci Swindoll, it is a time when we start believing anything is possible, regrets turn into challenges, defeats into lessons learned, and heartache into magnanimity.[25]And most importantly, just as the sun is most active in the natural season, so it seems that the Son of God appears to be most active in our life.

With all the summer season's glory, I would be remiss if I did not lift the cautionary warning that this can also become a dry season. It can be a time when our relaxation can become distorted, leaving us negligent in the disciplines that keep us closely connected to God. The enjoyment of the season can pull our attention far from the Source of life. The abundance of provision can become an overly desired pursuit, and the presence of prosperity can lure us into self-sufficiency. All of this can blind us to the need for continual feeding and lead us to a time of drought where the water of the Word becomes in short supply.

Of course, I do not share this admonition to create fear or burst the beautiful bubble of this strikingly peaceful and enjoyable season. I simply alert us to remember that although school may be out, we must keep learning. Although responsibilities are lifted, we must not become lazy. Although vacation is our current portion, we must know the difference between vacationing and vacating.

Have you ever gone on a really nice long vacation, yet toward the end, you find that you are ready to go home? That is because we were not designed to live in perpetual rest. The summer season of life is not intended to be an escape. It is a time of reprieve and retreat, where we enjoy the abundance of what has previously bloomed in our life. Relish the rest, savor the sights, embrace the enchantment, and welcome the warmth. And by all means, keep your eyes open to see the spectacular. It has been said that summer is the best season for seeing rainbows, and you certainly do not want to miss God's glorious show!

Season Thoughts

❖ What are some areas of your life where you are witnessing significant spiritual growth? In your emotional life? In your relational life?

❖ What are some of the lessons you learned and disciplines you employed in other seasons that have fortified you for your summer season?

❖ If you are not currently living in a summer season, what lessons do you need to learn and/or disciplines you need to employ to be prepared for your summer season?

❖ What cares might you be holding onto that may be hindering you from fully embracing what you know is a summer season of your life? What negative emotions might you need to address?

❖ List several ways you can ensure that your summer season does not become a time of spiritual drought.

❖ If you are currently in the summer season, in what ways can you share the brightness of your season as a means of encouragement for someone else?

Chapter Nine:
It's Harvest Time

I am a native of New York, and one of the most glorious experiences I can recall is when our small family would pack up the car for our annual ride upstate at the peak of fall. Even as a child, I could recognize that the changing colors of the leaves were a testament to the creative genius of God. Although I did not know it at the time, I was then and am now in complete agreement with Albert Camus, who said, "Autumn is a second spring, when every leaf is a flower."

It has been said, "Autumn is the season of contradictions. It is often associated with the melancholy of endings, yet it is the season of harvest and thanksgiving when we pause to count the blessings that have ripened from the seed we sowed the rest of the year."[26] Fall is indeed the season of harvest. After planting, watering, and waiting, the season ushers in the reward of reaping and enjoying the fruit of one's labors.

In both the Old and New Testaments, the word *harvest* is similarly defined as the time of and reaping the crop. Those simple definitions are encouraging, as they speak of both the period and the purpose. That which has been planted hears and heeds the alarm and knows it is time to bring forth the fullness of what it has to offer. Simultaneously, the harvester realizes that there is now an abundance that is available for enjoyment and use. Hence, harvest occurs in a specific period, and when it comes, the expectation is that one will realize and gain from that which has been previously planted.

Several years ago, I had to order replacement checks. (I realize there is an entire generation that may not even know what I am talking about here but stay with me!) The new order offered an opportunity to select predefined sayings that could be embossed under the signature line. Of the many available quotes, the one that caught my attention read, "Enjoy the fruits of your labor." I quickly selected that option, partially because I recognized those words as an excerpt from the Ecclesiastical writings but more so as a reminder that there was a season of my life when I could not spend as readily. This one succinct statement served as a declaration that the page had turned in my life. I had entered a new season, one for which there was greater abundance and additional resources at my disposal. Each time I signed a check, I was filled with a sense of gratitude for the harvest season that I was enjoying. Even though there was no guarantee of how long it would last, I knew that I was walking in my wealthy place.

The harvest season of life is a wealthy place. However, it is essential to clarify that wealth does not always materialize in the form of money. This can be the season of a wealth of peace, joy, rest, and gathering of both the simple and complex benefits of life. It is a time of being present when one can enjoy an abundance of good.

The harvest season of life is also a time of overflowing and thanksgiving. Much like the Jordan River in harvest time,[27] life seems to brim over with a profusion of what is needed for refreshing and cleansing. It can often be as though all the containments of life are released, and the waters of favor wash over us easily, leaving us full and fresh for each day's journey. And much like the American holiday, the harvest season of life seems to amplify the many reasons we have to give thanks. Our hearts are enraptured with a more profound sense of gratitude for even the most minor things, and we seem to be better equipped to see the many ways that we are blessed beyond measure.

As is the case for every season of life, this one contains a time for purpose to be accomplished—a truth that is probably more important to remember in the season of harvest than any other. I say that because more wisdom, restraint, and prayer are required in times of plenty than in times of shortage. In times when resources are limited, so are one's options. Our thoughts become centered around how to best appropriate what we have in our hands, often with the inner resolve that something will have to go lacking. Conversely, in times of plenty, choices are increased, and possibilities are boundless. It is no longer a matter of which option we will exercise, but how many we will take. Whether the supply is money, time, or skill, we must now exercise greater self-discipline and seek guidance on how the resource is to be used to fulfill the purpose for which it was made available.

This is when there is more than enough of life's goodness on hand. To rightly appropriate the purpose of the season, we must know what to do with our harvest and how best to use its richness for ourselves and others. So what is essential when in the harvest season of life? I believe there are three simple yet essential commitments we must make in our harvest season.

First, our harvest should be sampled. Listen to the voice of the Preacher: *"So I concluded there is nothing better than to be happy and enjoy ourselves as long as we can. And people should eat and drink and enjoy the fruits of their labor, for these are gifts from God."*[28] While the writer of Ecclesiastes is quoted differently in various biblical versions, the one phrase that remains consistent is that the fruits of our labor are gifts from God. The word *gift* is rendered from the Hebrew word *mattath* and is defined as a present or a reward.[29]

In agrarian cultures, oxen were used to stomp on the harvested grain to separate it from the chaff. During its labor, the oxen were to be allowed to eat some of the grain, thus partaking of the fruits of its labors. As a matter of fact, in the Old Testament, Moses forbade the Israelites from muzzling or preventing the animal from benefitting from what it was walking in.[30] Paul picked up this imagery when advocating for providing financial support for those who rendered spiritual service.[31]

In case you are scratching your head in wonderment, let me tie this together for you. If God cares about a beast of burden profiting from what it worked for, how much more does He want to present you with the gift of sampling the harvest you sowed? This is the season when you get to eat from what you worked on. Even if you have to dine in the presence of your enemies, harvest time is when you pull up a chair and partake of the rewards God is graciously giving to you.

Of course, all of life is a gift from God, but the harvest season is when special attention should be given to receiving and enjoying the benefits with deep gratitude. We must take time to sample the goodness of what God offers, embracing the psalmist's invitation by tasting and seeing that the Lord is good.[32] But while your prayers are being answered, your desires are being fulfilled, and your direction is being made clear, remember that your harvest should not only be sampled but it should also be saved.

The Proverbs writer used the industriousness of the ant to address the foolishness of lazy and passive humans. This insect was heralded for her wisdom in providing her bread in the summer and saving in her harvest.[33] The writer understood that the ebbs and flows of life guarantee that change is always on the horizon. This is in no way meant to be pessimistic, faithless, or throwing a wet blanket on the flaming embers of a blissfully abundant season. It is only to remind us of the cycles of life and to advocate for the wisdom of storing away some of the good that overtakes us during this glorious time. Just as we should never live on all of our income, we must maintain a residual of the gifts this season brings. In that way, we are assured of having something to undergird and sustain us when the season changes.

In addition to sampling and saving, we must be intentional about sharing our harvest. It appears to be God's pattern that everything He makes accessible in the harvest season is never intended for us only. Nowhere is this better demonstrated than in the pages of Leviticus. After a rescue mission from Egyptian bondage that would rival the most explosive action movie, God delivered His people through the miraculous parting of a sea, supernatural provision of food and water in a desert, and so much more. In preparation for obtaining the promises that God had made hundreds of years before, Moses taught the people through a series of codes concerning holiness, sacrifice, worship, and moral conduct regulations. Listen to God's plan for how His people were to handle their harvest:

> *When you harvest your crops, don't reap the corners of your fields, and don't pick up stray grains of wheat from the ground. It is the same with your grape crop-don't strip every last piece of fruit from the vines, and don't pick up the grapes that fall to the ground. Leave them for the poor and for those traveling through, for I am Jehovah your God.*[34]

More than 300 years later,[35] we find Boaz, the kinsman-redeemer, fulfilling the same mandate as he honored Ruth's faithfulness while she gleaned in his field. Boaz used not only the abundance of his wealth, but his power, standing, and influence to share with Ruth what would be enough for her needs, as well as the needs of her mother-in-law, Naomi. Boaz commanded the young men who harvested his fields to let grain from the bundles of sheaves fall purposely for her[36] and to let it remain. Boaz's kindness made it possible for Ruth to gather far more than what she could otherwise obtain.

Of course, most of us know how the story ends, but before we jump to redemption, let me bring us back to the point. When we are in the harvest season of life, we have the right to sample and the responsibility to save some of what is growing out of our lives. However, as we enjoy the fruit of our labors, we must be intentional about allowing some of the it to drop off, not because we were derelict in harvesting, but because we were mindful the harvest was meant to be shared.

While you enjoy the glories of such a powerful and abundant season, continue to be mindful of who may be benefited as you share from the residual and deep reservoir of the peace, joy, wisdom, grace, and insight you are walking in. This is the season to enjoy the fruits of your labors shamelessly, but it is also the season to allow others to eat from your garden. Those to whom you give a supply today may well be attached to the impact of the destiny you will see tomorrow. You never know; what you share from your current season may produce deliverance for someone in their next season.

Season Thoughts

❖ What comes to your mind when you think of harvest?

❖ Read Lev. 19:9-10, Lev. 23:22, and Deut. 24:19-22. What types of people were to benefit from the harvest of God's people? How does that correlate to the people who can be blessed from your season?

❖ What are some of the challenges you encounter when you are experiencing a season of abundance? What are some of the pitfalls you have to navigate during those times?

❖ In what ways do you find it difficult to sample, store, and share during the harvest of your life? What do you need to do to be better equipped to do all three in your next harvest season?

❖ Read the book of Ruth. Look at all the ways Boaz allowed Ruth to benefit from his influence. Look at how Ruth enabled Naomi to benefit from her increase. Now pray and ask God who you might intentionally share with during your season of harvest.

Chapter Ten:
Navigating the Corridors

It has been said that growth and change are synonymous and that it is often the initial signal that alerts us to a season of growth.[37] As I was working toward completing this book, I found that statement most true as I began navigating the journey from one season of my life to the next.

For the past thirty years, I have given my full attention, affection, and ability to the operations of New Covenant Christian Ministries, which is the church my husband and I started with only one member other than the two of us. Although I have worn a few different titles, Church Administrator, Co-Pastor, Executive Pastor, and Chief Operating Officer, the role has essentially been the same. I am responsible for assisting the Senior Pastor by overseeing the church's day-to-day operations, staff, and volunteers and recommending strategies for increased effectiveness and efficiency for church mission and vision alignment.

This is a role that has given me great fulfillment and one that I continue to enjoy. It has required a commitment to lifelong learning in several business disciplines and a great deal of time thinking linearly, logically, and strategically. I have learned so much and continue to use that knowledge to help other people develop in their ministerial and life call. But this commitment has also required that I live almost exclusively in my left brain, leaving me little time for creative thought and expression.

I now feel the winds of change blowing and the signs that I am moving into a new season of grace and gifting. I am turning the corner to more right-brain expressions and, while it does not mean that I have given up everything from the previous season, it does require that I deal with the trepidation that often accompanies change. My personal transition has encouraged me to close this work with a few insights that I am finding helpful for what I call the "corridors between seasons."

Although there is a set date on the calendar that designates the end of one season and the beginning of the next, rarely, if ever, do you see an immediate change. The cycle of seasons is determined by the tilt of the earth's axis toward the sun. Even though scientists and meteorologists can pinpoint this change, we who live on the planet may still be left experiencing weather patterns that look more like the closing season than the next. The point is that seasonal changes are rarely drastic; instead, they are transitional, giving us time to celebrate what we are leaving as we prepare for what is ahead.

We often say, "When one door closes, another opens," and I believe that to be true. But if you think about it, there must be a corridor for there to be two doors. The length and width of the passageway can and will vary, but there is always space between one door and the next. So the question that I am asking myself now, and one that I would recommend for your consideration as well, is, "How can I best navigate the corridor between where I am and the door to my next season?" Here are a few things that have come to my mind.

Expect some discomfort and maybe even a little fear. As a woman of faith, I unapologetically lean on the writings of Scripture and other authors to find insight, strength, instruction, and encouragement. What I most appreciate about both the Word of God and many writers' gifting is that some of the principles shared can apply equally whether or not one shares the same beliefs.

Such was the case when I read a statement written by Luci Swindoll about the emotion of fear. She said, "There resides in the heart of every believer a little pocket of fear. For some of us, it is cowardice. For others, it is timidity. Although we know the Savior gives courage and power, sometimes we feel safer in our little pocket than in His big provision."[38]

Despite your faith confession or lack thereof, most human beings would have to confess that change can be scary. Whether rooted in recognizing our true weakness or due to a perceived inability that we have accepted as real, change and transition require strength and courage. Even as I say this, I think about God's repeated encouragement to Joshua *to be strong and of good courage.*[39] Even the greatest, bravest, and most bold persons may need a bit of a pep talk before taking on the next season.

Navigating the corridor of seasonal change can bring about a degree of angst. It is crucial to expect the discomfort, but it is equally vital that we be honest about our feelings of apprehension and maybe even foreboding.

What made Superman so appealing was not just his strength. It was the fact that he was nothing more than Clark

Kent imbued with supernatural power. And that is precisely what will help those within our sphere of influence be empowered—when we are honest about the challenges we face as we step out of one door of life and begin the corridor journey to the next. Showing others that we are nothing more than ordinary people who trust in a supernatural strength to face our fears will be the catalyst for ourselves and the example for others. As it has been said, "The richest testimonies come from people He has made whole and who still remember what it was like to be broken."[40] This means that we cannot live in isolation, regardless of the season, only allowing people to see us in the good times. We must be willing to tell the whole truth—sharing the good and the not-so-good. We must have the resolve to understand that our brokenness is a better bridge for people than our pretend wholeness could ever be.[41]

Be confident that you already have everything needed for the next season of your life. In the opening of his second letter, the Apostle Peter says, *"By his divine power, God has given us everything we need for living a godly life."* [42] No limits. No time constraints. No end-clauses. He posits no qualifiers of duration or potential expirations—simply that God gives us everything we need!

If that is not sufficient encouragement, Moses puts the icing on the cake in Deut. 31:7-8: *Then Moses called Joshua and said to him in the sight of all Israel, "Be strong and of good courage, for you must go with this people to the land which the Lord has sworn to their fathers to give them, and you shall cause them to inherit it. And the Lord, He is the One who goes before you. He will be with you. He will not leave you nor forsake you; do not fear nor be dismayed."*

Each time I read these passages, my confidence is bolstered. I do not revel in my abilities but in the belief that God is always ahead of me, ushering me into what He has already determined is for me. Please excuse me while I take a moment to rejoice for both of us!

I once heard Bishop Joseph Garlington say, "God does not judge you on where you are, but on what you refuse to become." I pondered that statement long after he said it, and the days and weeks that followed gave me a deeper understanding of its meaning. Our responsibility is to have confidence that God will not direct us into a future for which we are ill-equipped. While I believe that we should never become so self-reliant that we think we can accomplish anything on our own, there must always be an unshakable belief in the sovereignty of the Way Maker. We must have an unwavering acceptance that who we are and what we possess is more than enough for both the journey and the destination. That is the lens through which we must view both our now and our next, all while being fully convinced that the one who began a good work in us will perform it.[43]

Know that your age does not hinder God's purpose. I came across this quote during one of my morning devotionals: *"Society may glamorize youth and marginalize age, but your season of life does not limit God."*[44] I still remember dropping my journal and breaking down in tears when I read that short statement. You see, like so many others, I, too, have found myself fighting the voices in my mind that were saying, "You are too late." "If it has not happened yet, what makes you think it will ever happen?" "Why would you even consider leaving the comfort of what you are doing to embark on something else?"

The Apostle Paul addressed the same issue from a different vantage point when he spoke to his spiritual son, Timothy: *Let no one despise your youth, but be an example to the believers in word, in conduct, in love, in spirit, in faith, in purity.*[45] In this case, his encouragement spoke to a younger man who needed reminding that the effectiveness of his purpose could not be diminished by the shortage of his chronological years.

Whether you are just starting in life's journey or have been walking the path for many years, the point remains the same. Age cannot be superimposed over the seasons of life, nor can age be seen as a shield from the issues that come with those seasons. Young or old, you will find yourself in varying seasons. In each one, you must know that God's purpose can and will prevail. Despite what society and others may say, you must realize that you are never too young or too old to fulfill the purpose for the seasons of your life. If we cannot control a season, we need not worry about whether our age qualifies us to walk fully in one. Our only responsibility is to give way to God's purpose.

If you are young, dream big and embrace the opportunities that are being afforded you. If you are more mature, reconnect with your passion. No matter how busy life has become since that dream first took root in your heart and no matter how impossible it may seem under the current circumstances of your life, let it come alive again. Begin to think about it; begin to pray about it; begin to take steps in its direction, even if they are small.[46]

Seek, find, and live out the significance of every season. A few years ago, I began hosting an annual conference for women that centers around the theme of building a life of significance. As I prepared for one of the events, the thought of legacy came to my mind. During our planning, my team and I decided to give framed quotes to each attendee to remind them of the importance of moving from just seeking success to living lives of significance. One of the quotes was from the legendary Jackie Robinson, who broke the color barrier to become the first African American to play in Major League Baseball. He said, *"A life isn't significant except for its impact on others."* The truth of these words would not be lost on anyone who even remotely understands the magnitude of his accomplishment on the game of baseball, the city of Brooklyn, New York in 1947, and on the world of sports at large.

Mr. Robinson's words help to confirm that every season of life affords us opportunities to impact others. Whether times are cold or warm, times of sowing, or times of reaping, we each have a responsibility to use our season as an opportunity to break through barriers for ourselves and be a source of strength and encouragement for others. Our passage through the corridor of transition should allow us time to consider how we will use the next season's resources and opportunities to become a better version of ourselves. Success is great, but significance, living out the meaning and worth of our lives, is of more value than any position or title we can acquire. In the words of Dr. Samuel R. Chand, renowned leadership and dream coach, "Legacy is a life-long project defined by how you impart into the lives of others."

In every season, we must be committed to living lives of significance. Such a life should never be confused with only accomplishing big things or achieving notoriety. It is living from an authentic self in which the layers on the outside are merely expressions of the core on the inside.[47] Or, as Edmund Chan said, "It is not the important things we do that make a significant life; rather, it is a significant life that makes what we do important."[48]

Final Thoughts

It is only now that I have come to realize that this work and labor of love has been as much for me as it has been for you, dear reader. I hope that as you embrace your current season or navigate the corridor of transition into your next, that you will make the commitment that I have grasped during this time. I pray that you will traverse the seasons of your life with eyes of anticipation and not dread and that you will join me in looking for the legacy opportunity beyond the next door.

Maximizing the seasons of our lives will require prayerful reflection of who we must bring in, who we must build up, and who we must birth out. We must be intentional about seeing the strength and beauty of the women God brings in our lives, building them up with our words and our presence. It is a truth that when we mother and mentor others, we create an imperishable legacy that lives on long after we are gone to be with our Father.[49]

As I consider the seasons of my own life, I have embraced that my ceiling must become another woman's floor. I must give her the platform to go higher by enabling her to start where I already am. I trust that you will contemplate how you can do the same for those within your sphere of influence, those who have been intentionally placed within arm's reach of your life.

Finally, my sincerest hope is that this will be a resource to which you will return regularly and share unselfishly. In every season, may we be found searching for the chance to share what we have learned to encourage others with what we have experienced and expend our relational equity on behalf of those who will use it to navigate their seasons with grace.

May you always be found living in the overflow!

Dr. D'

About the Author

A native of Brooklyn, New York, Dr. D'Ann V. Johnson is a licensed and ordained minister with over thirty years of ministerial experience. She has earned a B.A. in Biblical Education, an M.A. in Christian Education, and a D. Min. with a concentration in Discipleship and Leadership.

In 1994 she left a corporate position as a course developer and executive trainer to assume a full-time position with New Covenant Christian Ministries, the church she co-founded with her husband in 1991. Her current position as Executive Pastor includes sharing in the teaching and preaching rotation and overseeing the church's day-to-day operations and its staff. Beyond her church duties, Dr. D', as she is affectionately known, expresses her commitment to the educational community by serving on the Board of Trustees of Beulah Heights University in Atlanta, Georgia. She has also been a guest instructor at Luther Rice Seminary, teaching Church Administration & Management.

Dr. D' expanded her ministry by becoming the founder and president of three distinct organizations: *Overflow Ministries*, designed to disciple, mentor, and strengthen women in their life call and purpose; *Administrative Resource Consultants* developed to support churches in business operations and administrative staff training; and *Psalmist &*

Scribe Publishing, a company dedicated to the promotion of the gospel message through the production of written and musical compositions. Dr. D's first self-published works include a devotional guide entitled *Notes from My Bible*; the mini-book, *Keys to a Leader's Success*; the book, *What to do When You're Going Through*; and her latest work, *The Seasons of a Woman's Life.*

Dr. D' is a woman who maintains a consistent life of devotion and a solid walk with the Lord. She is the loving wife to Pastor Billy R. Johnson and a devoted mother to their adult son, Stephen Darius.

An inspiring and well-respected servant, this woman willingly shares her gifts with the body of Christ. Whether she is ministering God's Word, training church leaders, teaching administrative principles, or ministering to women, Dr. D'Ann Johnson works diligently to share with others the key to doing the work of the ministry in excellence.

D'Ann V. Johnson

Endnotes:

Chapter 1

1 Dictionary.com. *Stage,* noun.

2 Ecclesiastes 3:1

3 Biblesoft's New Exhaustive Strong's Numbers and Concordance with Expanded Greek-Hebrew Dictionary. Copyright © 1994, 2003, 2006 Biblesoft, Inc. and International Bible Translators, Inc. OT:2165 *zeman.*

4 Biblesoft's New Exhaustive Strong's Numbers and Concordance. OT:2163 *zaman.*

5 Ibid, OT2656; OT:2654.

Chapter 2

6 Moore, Beth. *The Beloved Disciple.* 2003, B&H Books. Kindle Edition, page 116.

Chapter 3

7 Mr. Derrick Adams of The Adams Group has been our landscaper now for over twenty years. I continue to be impressed by his meticulous eye for the beauty of God's creation, and I am grateful for ongoing kindness.

8 Proverbs 16:9; 10:21

9 Daniel 2:20-21a

10 Walsh, Sheila. *Giving God Your Future Bible Study Series* by Christa Kinde. 2006, Thomas Nelson Publishers, page 21.

Chapter 4

11 Genesis 8:22

12 Proverbs 20:4

83

Chapter 5

[13] Our Daily Bread, December 31, 2008.

[14] Van Tongeren, Daryl R. Ph.D. *The Seasons of Life, or How to Survive Life's Winter Moments.* https://www.psychologytoday.com/us/blog/meaning-making/201502/the-seasons-life-or-how-survive-lifes-winter-moments. Posted Feb 24, 2015.

Chapter 6

[15] Biblesoft's New Exhaustive Strong's Numbers and Concordance. OT:2779 *choreph*; OT:2778 *charaph*.

[16] Walsh, Sheila. *The Storm Inside: Trade the Chaos of How You Feel for the Truth of Who You Are.*

[17] Moore, Beth. *The Beloved Disciple.* 2003, B&H Books, Kindle Edition, pg. 220.

[18] Clairmont, Patsy. *Giving God Your Future Bible Study Series* by Christa Kinde. 2005, Thomas Nelson Publishers, page 79.

[19] Stein, Traci Ph.D., MPH, *"Winter Rage," Mindfulness, and the Gift of the Present.* https://www.psychologytoday.com/us/blog/the-integrationist/201403/winter-rage-mindfulness-and-the-gift-the-present. Posted Mar 05, 2014.

[20] Song of Solomon 2:11-13a English Standard Version.

[21] The Passover, a commemoration of Israel's deliverance from Egyptian bondage, is celebrated in the month of Nisan (also called Abib), which is March-April. This marks the new year because it was the beginning of Israel's new life as a people.

[22] Scioli, Anthony. *Why Spring Is the Season of Hope: Hope Springs Eternal.* https://www.psychologytoday.com/us/blog/hope-today/201203/why-spring-is-the-season-hope.

[23] Wiersbe, Warren. *Be Alive,* page 147.

[24] An insight shared by Joanne Hudson during one of our small group sessions.

D'Ann V. Johnson

Chapter 8

[25] Swindoll, Luci. *Doing Life Differently: The Art of Living with Imagination.*

Chapter 9

[26] Bernhard J.D., Toni. *Autumn's Fullness and Beauty: Quotations and Photographs.* https://www.psychologytoday.com/us/blog/turning-straw-gold/201311/autumns-fullness-and-beauty-quotations-and-photographs. Posted Nov. 17, 2013.

[27] Joshua 3:14-16

[28] Ecclesiastes 3:12-13. Holy Bible, New Living Translation ®, copyright © 1996, 2004 by Tyndale Charitable Trust. Used by permission of Tyndale House Publishers. All rights reserved.

[29] Biblesoft's New Exhaustive Strong's Numbers and Concordance with Expanded Greek-Hebrew Dictionary. Copyright © 1994, 2003, 2006 Biblesoft, Inc. and International Bible Translators, Inc.) OT:4991 *matath.*

[30] Deuteronomy 25:4

[31] 1 Timothy 5:17-18

[32] Psalm 34:8

[33] Proverbs 6:6-8

[34] Leviticus 19:9-10. The Living Bible.

[35] https://biblehub.com/timeline/old.htm.

[36] Ruth 2:1-18.

Chapter 10

[37] Clairmont, Patsy. *Giving God Your Future Bible Study Series* by Christa Kinde. 2005, Thomas Nelson Publishers, page 74.

[38] Swindoll, Luci. *Giving God Your Future Bible Study Series* by Christa Kinde. 2005, Thomas Nelson Publishers, page 39.

[39] Joshua 1:6, 7, 9

[40] Moore, Beth. *Breaking Free Day by Day.* 2007, B&H Publishing Group. Kindle Edition, page 35.

[41] Walsh, Sheila. *https://www.goodreads.com/author/quotes/21763.Sheila_Walsh*.

[42] Holy Bible, New Living Translation ®, copyright © 1996, 2004 by Tyndale Charitable Trust. Tyndale House Publishers, 2 Peter 1:3a

[43] Philippians 1:6

[44] *The Word for You Today.* January 1, 2019.

[45] 1 Timothy 4:12

[46] Moody, Van. *The I Factor: How Building a Great Relationship with Yourself Is the Key to a Happy, Successful Life.* 2016, Thomas Nelson Publishers. Kindle Edition.

[47] Johnson, Nicole. *Fresh-Brewed Life Revised & Updated: A Stirring Invitation to Wake Up Your Soul.*

[48] Chan, Edmund. *Cultivating Your Inner Life: Reflections on Spiritual Formation in Discipleship Today.* E-book.

Final Thoughts

[49] Jakes, Serita. *Beside Every Good Man: Loving Myself While Standing by Him.* 2008, FaithWords. Kindle Edition, location 3026.

D'Ann V. Johnson

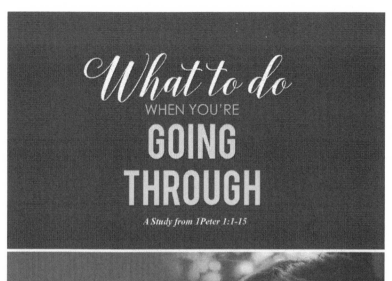

What to do
WHEN YOU'RE
GOING
THROUGH

A Study from 1Peter 1:1-15

What to do When You're Going Through combines the scriptural backdrop of 1 Peter 1:1-15 with real life examples of God's sufficient love and then weaves them into wisdom for the journey through life's hard places.

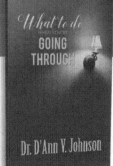

As you read, you will discover principles that will strengthen you along the path and lead you to a victorious end.

www.liveintheoverflow.org

The Seasons Of A Woman's Life

A Devotional Guide to Enhance Your Time With God

Notes From My Bible

Notes From My Bible by Dr. D'Ann V. Johnson is a devotional guide designed to enhance your time with God. This compilation of thoughts and prayers will serve to encourage, strengthen, and inspire its readers. The power of God's Word coupled with the insightful messages will change your life and lead you into the presence of God.

Designed to be used interactively, each written devotional is supported by a scriptural reference and pictorial illustration, and then followed by a journal page for personal notes. This unique assemblage will motivate you to read your Bible in a fresh and different way, and will encourage you to develop a renewed love for God and His Word.

Order Today...

OTHER RESOURCES

For other resources from Dr. D, please visit
www.liveintheoverflow.org, your source
for scriptually sound principles and life
skills that encourge and enhance a strong
and vital relationship with the Lord.

FOLLOW US  @overflowministries

 @drdvjohnson

 @drdvjohnson

 @overflowministriesintl

Made in the USA
Columbia, SC
24 June 2021